Riding High

Bruce C. Rucker Sr.

Published by:

Global Books Publishers

ISBN: 978-1-970816-10-5

DEDICATION

To my wife, whose unwavering love has been the shining light in the darkest moments of my life. Your faith in me, even when I was lost, held me together and allowed me to see the man I could become.

To my four children, who witnessed my struggles and now share in the beauty of our renewed relationship. I am grateful for your understanding, your forgiveness, and your love.

And *to God,* the God of second chances, who granted me the grace to redeem myself and guided me from despair to hope.

May this story stand as a testament to the power of love, faith, and the possibility of new beginnings for all who seek them.

ACKNOWLEDGEMENTS

First and foremost, I give thanks to God, the God of second chances, for guiding me from darkness into light and for granting me the strength to begin anew. Without divine grace and mercy, this journey would not have been possible.

To my wife, whose unwavering love and faith have been my anchor in the storm. Your support, patience, and belief in me, even when I was lost, held me together and inspired me to become the person I am today.

To my four children, who have witnessed my struggles and now share in the beauty of our restored relationship, I am grateful for your understanding and love. You are my greatest blessings.

To my parents in Heaven and my family, thank you for your encouragement and for never giving up on me. Your guidance and prayers were instrumental in my becoming an overcomer.

To my fellowship family and friends, especially those who walked alongside me during my spiritual ascent, your kindness, honesty, and support have been a source of strength and hope.

To all those in the trucking community, mentors, and colleagues who believed in my potential and helped me rediscover my purpose, your trust and camaraderie have enriched my life and career.

To everyone who has shared their own stories of overcoming adversity, thank you for reminding me that we are never alone in our struggles. May this book encourage you to embrace hope, seek help, and trust in your ability to overcome.

Finally, to Amelia Taylor for the beautiful cover design, and to all who contributed to the creation of this book, your talents and dedication are deeply appreciated.

With heartfelt gratitude,

Bruce C. Rucker Sr.

Table of Contents

INTRODUCTION

"Riding High" is a deeply personal and inspiring journey of transformation, resilience, and faith. In these pages, Bruce C. Rucker Sr. invites readers into the heart of his story. A story marked by struggle, redemption, and the pursuit of authentic joy. From the challenges of growing up as a middle child, through the dark valleys of addiction, to the triumphs of recovery and spiritual renewal, this memoir is a testament to the power of perseverance and the grace of second chances.

The narrative is honest and unflinching, exploring the realities of addiction and the toll it takes on relationships, self-worth, and purpose. Yet, at its core, it is a story of hope. Through faith, community, and a relentless desire to change, Bruce discovers that the journey to "riding high" is not about fleeting highs or external validation, but about finding peace, gratitude, and meaning in everyday life.

This book is more than a memoir. It is a guide for anyone seeking transformation. Each chapter concludes with thoughtful journal reflections, encouraging readers to pause, reflect, and engage with their own stories of overcoming adversity. Whether you are facing your own struggles or supporting someone on their path to recovery, this work offers wisdom, encouragement, and the assurance that no matter how dark the past may have been, a brighter future is possible.

May this story inspire you to embrace hope, pursue your purpose, and discover what it truly means to ride high on life's true current.

CHAPTER 1:

ORIGIN

My early life mirrored my internal struggles. Being neither the oldest nor the youngest, I was instead in the steadfast middle, often overlooked, expected to adapt and endure. Despite these challenges, I persevered, finding solace in friendships and moments of personal accomplishment. This came mostly in high school when I was a Gentry singer and participated in a school play. My school years encompass good memories of going from learner to practitioner. I graduated from high school and went on to earn an Associate's degree, a symbol of both resilience and the beginning of a new chapter.

With a diploma in hand, I set out to explore the professional world. My career path has been vast and varied. Not long after graduating from college, I relocated to Los Angeles, California. A city alive with possibility, yet equally capable of overwhelming those searching for stability. It was in Los Angeles that I met my first wife. We had two boys together. They are now men with their own accomplishments and families. I thank their mother for the outstanding job she did, taking them from boys to men.

I secured a position at a well-known cosmetic company where I compounded chemicals. I was what they called a chemical compounder. While working there, I began to make drugs with chemicals and found myself getting high from the fumes. Addiction rarely announces itself with fanfare; instead, it creeps in silently until one day you find yourself lost in a trap. The descent had started.

Honestly, when I first started using drugs, it did not seem important. It was just something I did with friends to feel like I belonged and to quiet the constant noise of self-doubt in my head. I kept telling myself, "Just one last time, and I will quit." However, the truth is that it took me 22 years to quit, until I was "riding high."

After leaving the cosmetic company due to a layoff, I became employed with a major airline. We would later move with the company, and I would lose that job due to my addiction. At this point, I decided to change focus. Our next destination was Oklahoma. There is something about going home. With newfound clarity, and with the help of my parents, I enrolled in truck driving school. It was a decision rooted in both necessity and the appeal of the open road. I graduated from truck driving school, completed my training, and earned my Commercial Driving License. The diverse roles I occupied showed my adaptability and work ethic.

Each job presented new challenges, unfamiliar faces, and the opportunity to redefine myself. The steady rhythm of the highway, the responsibility of transporting goods across the country, and the independence of the profession suited me well. Yet beneath the surface, my internal struggles lingered. The quest for belonging, a thread woven through my childhood, remained unresolved. I was always searching for meaning and purpose. I found myself "riding high."

During this search, I encountered a force that would come to redefine my life: addiction. What began as experimentation or an escape soon escalated into a consuming dependency. As the addiction tightened its grip, every aspect of my life began to unravel. At first, I tried to manage my habit by convincing myself that I was still in control. But addiction crept into my career, my marriage, and my image. Money that should have gone toward rent payments, food, and necessities, I spent on feeding an ever-growing habit that demanded more to achieve the same effect. The consequences of my actions began to accumulate, and I found myself isolated, ashamed, and uncertain of a way out. Family ties strained under the weight of my addiction. My first marriage ended in divorce. I grew increasingly secretive and unreliable.

I became an expert in deception, crafting elaborate stories to explain away my behavior, my appearance, and my frequent absences. I learned to function while riding high, to appear normal when I was anything but, and to manipulate the people who cared about me most. Unbeknownst to my sister, I often borrowed money from her to feed my addiction. The guilt from these deceptions only deepened my need to escape, creating a vicious cycle that seemed impossible to break. But God is so amazing! My children never had to witness me getting high, and I thank God they did not follow my pattern.

I regained my footing and worked hard to mend my relationships. Although my first marriage ended, over time, I found love again and married a partner who accepted both my struggles and hopes for the future. Together, we formed a blended family with two daughters, creating a home filled with acceptance, understanding, and growth.

For most people, the story would have ended there. But my journey was far from over. My new soul mate also had to endure my struggle with drugs for a period. Raised in the church, I had known the comfort of faith. I remember sermons that resonated with hope, communal singing that lifted spirits, and the quiet assurance that, in God's eyes, everyone is valued. Yet, as my addiction deepened, I drifted from those early teachings. I felt alienated, not just from my loved ones but from God and myself.

This is my story of my descent into a mysterious world of addiction, where I found myself "riding high." Amazingly, and more importantly, it is the story of my ascent with God leading the charge to a position of "riding high" His way. The truth is, God took me from someplace, to a no place, to a new place.

REFLECTIONS

Take a moment to reflect on your own journey. Use the prompts below
to guide your thoughts:

My Early Life

1. *What aspects of your childhood or upbringing shaped who you are today?*

____

____

____

____

2. *Were there moments when you felt overlooked or had to adapt and endure?*

____

____

____

____

3. *Write about a memory that stands out.*

____

____

____

____

Personal Accomplishments

1.   Recall a time when you achieved something meaningful, even if it seemed small.

____

____

____

____

2.   How did it make you feel?

____

____

____

3.   What did you learn from that experience?

____

____

____

____

Transitions

1. *Think about a major transition in your life (school, career, relationships, or moving to a new place).*

---

2. *What challenges did you face? How did you persevere?*

Resilience

1. *In what ways have you shown resilience in the face of adversity?*

---

2. *What helped you keep going?*

____

____

____

____

Looking Forward

1. *What new chapter are you hoping to begin?*

____

____

____

____

2. *What steps can you take to move toward it?*

____

____

____

____

CHAPTER 2:

EXODUS

At this point, the possibility of redemption emerged. Desperate for change, I found myself returning to the Church, first hesitantly, then with growing conviction. The rhythm of worship, the warmth of fellowship, and the teachings of faith began to rekindle a sense of hope within me. I rededicated my life to Christ, surrendering my struggle and seeking strength beyond my own.

This renewed faith became the cornerstone of my Exodus. With my wife's help, I confronted my addiction head-on. I did it without any treatment or counseling. I stopped completely. I was tired of being sick and tired. What helped me stop was when I felt like I was having a heart attack once, as a reaction to the drugs. Jesus saved me that night. I committed right then and there that it was my exodus from drugs. For change to occur, I had to act. It was driven by a stronger incentive that outweighed the reason for me to stay the same. That involved me taking the first step, though small, to break old habits and build momentum toward a desired future vision. Change, I learned, starts within.

The process was neither quick nor easy, but each hard-won victory brought with it a sense of restoration and self-forgiveness. Drug addiction is the shadow that often sneaks into the corners of a life unnoticed, only to consume its host with relentless force. My story is not unique in its struggle, but it stands as a testament to the power of faith and the transforming light found in scripture. This account is not just about battling addiction, but about the spiritual awakening that led me out of darkness and into a life rebuilt upon biblical truth. The self-help method may not work for everyone. I am not suggesting everyone can stop on their own. Please get professional help or join a support group if you need it.

My journey from addiction to overcoming instilled in me a profound sense of purpose. No longer content with my own victory over addiction, I felt called to share my story and support others facing similar struggles. I started combining my lived experience with my passion for service. I spend time witnessing with others in the community, particularly those battling addiction. I speak openly about the realities of substance abuse, the devastation it brings, and the hope that can be found in Jesus Christ.

My story is one of perseverance, redemption, and the transformative power of faith. From a childhood spent searching for belonging as a middle child, through years of struggle and self-doubt, to the dark depths of addiction and the bright horizon of recovery, my life bears witness to the possibility of change. I learned it is all in the thought process. Remember that our past does not define our future, that setbacks can become stepping-stones, and that with faith and support, even the deepest wounds can heal.

Nobody chooses to become an addict overnight. My own story began casually, as I mentioned. I was simply trying to fit in, ease my anxiety, and feel less invisible. When with friends, someone might pass something around, and I would think, "Why not?" At first, it seemed harmless. I convinced myself I was just relaxing and that I could quit anytime.

Drug addiction via crack cocaine is a chapter filled with shame and regret, but it is also a story of awakening. Admitting addiction marked the beginning of my journey toward my exodus from drugs. Though the scars remained, I have learned that healing starts with honesty and a willingness to change. Rock bottom is a turning point. It is where the healing journey begins and where hope is reborn.

No matter how dark the past, the future holds the promise of renewal, growth, and a life filled with meaning. Overcoming addiction has changed me in ways I could never have foreseen. I am more empathetic, patient, and grateful. I am so incredibly grateful to God for His unconditional love for me and for His redeeming the time, and restoring everything I had let the devil steal. There is no question of God's greatness, and His mercy is everlasting! God gave me back double for my trouble.

I thank God I am in my right mind and do not look like what I have been through. The residue is not on me. Hallelujah! It was the stinking thinking causing the problem. I had to let go and let God. I am not defined by my addiction, nor by the mistakes I made during its reign. Overcoming is now my testament to the strength that lies within all of us. There will be setbacks, but each day is a new chance to choose hope over despair. Surround yourself with people who understand, seek professional guidance if needed, and build routines that nurture your physical and emotional well-being. Most importantly, believe that change is possible.

The road is long, but becoming an overcomer is worth it. My journey from addiction to being an overcomer has been hard, but every hardship has shaped me into someone stronger, wiser, and more compassionate.

The damage is behind me. God has erased it. I have made many mistakes in life. But as Wolfgang Riebe once said regarding mistakes: "That is why pencils have erasers." We all make errors in our lives. No person is immune to error. Thank God for erasers! Life after addiction is not perfect, but it is authentic, and it is mine.

For anyone reading this, may my story encourage you to take the exodus from addiction, embrace hope, and trust your ability to overcome. In the depths of darkness, there is always a glimmer of light, sometimes faint, sometimes dazzling, and with courage, you can follow it to a new beginning.

Rock Bottom & Turning Points

1. *Can you recall a moment when you felt you had reached your lowest point? What thoughts or feelings did you experience at that time?*

____

____

____

____

2. *What was the catalyst that inspired you to seek change or redemption?*

____

____

____

____

Faith and Renewal

1. *Have you ever returned to a source of comfort or faith during a difficult period? What role did spirituality, community, or belief play in your healing process?*

____

____

____

____

2. *How did reconnecting with faith or supportive people help you begin your journey of recovery?*

____

____

____

____

Confronting Challenges

1. *What steps did you take (or could you take) to confront a personal struggle head-on?*

____

____

____

2. *Who or what supported you most during this process? How did their support impact your journey?*

____

____

____

____

Purpose and Service

1. *Has overcoming adversity given you a new sense of purpose or desire to help others?*

____

____

____

____

2. *In what ways have you (or could you) used your experiences to support or encourage others facing similar challenges?*

____

____

____

____

Transformation and Identity

1. *How has your identity changed because of overcoming a major challenge?*

____

____

____

____

2. *What qualities (such as empathy, patience, or gratitude) have you developed through your journey?*

____

____

____

____

Hope and Moving Forward

1. *What does hope mean to you now, compared to before your transformation?*

____

____

____

____

2. *What advice would you give to someone who is currently struggling, based on your own experience?*

____

____

____

____

Chapter 3:

Hope

Addiction can be one of the darkest valleys a person may walk through. Whether it is substance abuse, gambling, or destructive behaviors, the grip of addiction often leads to despair, isolation, and broken relationships. Yet, within the sacred texts of the Bible, hope shines as an unwavering light, offering comfort and direction for those struggling with addiction. I, too, found solace in reading scriptures and meditating on them.

Scripture reminds us that God's plans for us offer hope and restoration. As Jeremiah 29:11 declares, "For I know the thoughts that I think toward you, says the Lord, thoughts of peace and not of evil, to give you a future and a hope." Even in moments of deep struggle, this promise assures us that our story is not over and that God's love can guide us toward healing.

My entire journey through addiction generated feelings of hopelessness. The psalmist expresses hopelessness in Psalm 42:11: "Why are you cast down, O my soul? And why are you disquieted within me? Hope in God; For I shall yet praise Him, the help of my countenance and my God." This verse encourages those in despair to turn their hearts toward God, trusting that hope can be found even in the darkest times. I found this to be true. It helped me in the dark hours of my life.

Lamentations 3:21-23 reminds us, "This I recall to my mind. Therefore, have hope. Through the Lord's mercies we are not consumed, because His compassions fail not. They are new every morning; Great is Your faithfulness." Remember, each day brings new opportunities for grace and renewal.

For those feeling weary in their battle, Isaiah 40:31 offers reassurance: "But those who wait on the Lord shall renew their strength; They shall mount up with wings like eagles, they shall run and not grow weary, they shall walk and not be faint." God's strength is available to all who seek Him, empowering them to persevere. He can take you through it and to a new place.

As you continue reading, may these scriptures serve as 911 numbers for your soul, as Hebrews 6:19 says: "This hope we have as an anchor of the soul, both sure and steadfast, and which enters the presence beyond the veil." Through faith, hope becomes a powerful force that leads to transformation, restoration, and peace.

Addiction often feels like a journey through a shadowed valley, where hope seems distant and the future uncertain. Yet, the Bible assures us that suffering is not the end of our story. Romans 5:3-5 teaches, "And not only that, but we also glory in tribulations, knowing that tribulation produces perseverance, and perseverance, character, and character, hope. Now hope does not disappoint, because the love of God has been poured out in our hearts by the Holy Spirit who was given to us." Even when experiencing pain, God is at work, shaping us and pouring His love into our hearts.

Overcoming addiction requires strength that often feels beyond our own capacity. Isaiah 40:31 offers encouragement: "But those who wait on the Lord shall renew their strength. They shall mount up with wings like eagles. They shall run and not be weary, and they shall walk and not faint." This promise reminds us that God's strength is available to those who seek Him, and that renewal is possible even when we feel it is impossible. This assurance is a beacon for anyone feeling lost, reminding us that God's vision for our lives offers restoration and purpose.

Hope is not passive; it is an anchor that keeps us steady. Hebrews 6:19 says, "This hope we have as an anchor of the soul, both sure and steadfast, and which enters the presence behind the veil, where the forerunner has entered for us, even Jesus, having become High Priest according to the order of Melchizedek." In moments of temptation or doubt, hope rooted in God's promises keeps us grounded and focused on the path to recovery.

Addiction may cast a long shadow, but the light of hope found in scripture can guide us through the darkness. As Romans 15:13 encourages, "Now may the God of hope fill you with all joy and peace in believing, that you may abound in hope by the power of the Holy Spirit." Through faith, perseverance, and trust in God's promises, healing and restoration are possible. I am living proof of this hope we have through Jesus Christ. My soul is now anchored in the Lord!

Thank God I am riding high His way now! My station in life now reminds me of my favorite recording artist, Frankie Beverly, and some of his songs. "Through the joys and pains of life and all the happy feelings, there is a golden time of day."

Defining Hope in Darkness

1. *When have you felt hopeless or trapped by an inconvenient situation? What thoughts or emotions did you experience during that time?*

____

____

____

____

2. *What helped you hold onto hope, even when things seemed bleak?*

____

____

____

Scriptural Anchors

1. *Is there a particular scripture or spiritual teaching that has given you comfort or direction during a struggle?*

____

____

____

2. *How do these words influence your outlook on recovery and healing?*

____

____

____

Renewed Strength

1. *Can you recall a time when you felt renewed strength or perseverance in your journey? What contributed to this renewal?*

____

____

____

____

2. *How did faith, community, or personal determination play a role?*

____

____

____

____

Daily Renewal

1.   What does "new mercies every morning" mean to you in your own life?

____

____

____

____

2.   How do you practice letting go of yesterday's mistakes and embracing each new day?

____

____

____

____

God's Plans and Your Future

1.   How do you interpret the idea that God has "plans to give you hope and a future"?

____

____

____

____

2. In what ways do you see your life moving toward restoration and purpose?

____

____

____

Hope as an Anchor

1. What anchors you when you feel tempted or discouraged?

____

____

____

2. How do you stay grounded in hope during moments of doubt or struggle?

____

____

____

Transformation through Suffering

1. *How has suffering or adversity shaped your character and sense of hope?*

____

____

____

____

2. *What qualities have you developed through your journey of overcoming addiction or hardship?*

____

____

____

____

Sharing Hope

1. *How can you use your story or expériences to encourage others who may be struggling?*

____

____

____

____

2. *What message of hope would you share with someone who feels lost or defeated?*

____

____

____

____

CHAPTER 4:

OVERCOMING

I regained my focus, and a deep-rooted desire for meaning in life resurfaced. I found myself drawn back to familiar passages of the Bible. The stories of perseverance, of flawed individuals finding redemption, resonated deeply with my own struggle. The Psalms became a daily refuge. They were my constant companions during the days of overcoming addiction. David's honesty about his struggles, his willingness to cry out to God in anger and desperation, and his ultimate trust in divine faithfulness resonated deeply with my own experience. Psalm 40 became particularly meaningful. Having been pulled by God from the pit of addiction and placed on the solid ground of recovery was phenomenal.

The scriptures reminded me that it was not the result of my own strength or willpower, but of God's grace and mercy. This understanding was crucial to my overcoming addiction. God was doing the heavy lifting. The New Testament passage about redemption helped me stay grounded as I progressed in overcoming addiction. 2 Corinthians 5:17 became my life source: "Therefore, if anyone is in Christ, he is a new creation; old things have passed away; behold, all things have become new." This promise gave me hope that I was not defined by my past forever, but could become someone entirely new through God's transforming power.

When cravings hit, I began to memorize scripture verses that spoke directly to my struggles with addiction and overcoming. I would recite Philippians 4:13: "I can do all things through Christ who strengthens me." When shame threatened to overwhelm me, I would remember

Romans 8:1: "Therefore, there is no condemnation to those who are in Christ Jesus." When I felt alone and abandoned, I would cling to Hebrews 13:5: "I will never leave you nor forsake you." The Word became a weapon to defeat the lies of the devil. The Word proved to be sharper than any two-edged sword, rightly dividing the Word of truth.

I began to have a personal relationship with God again. I moved beyond rote prayers to genuine conversations. My fellowship family has been a blessing in my spiritual journey. The practice of gratitude became an integral part of my spiritual discipline. In my addiction years, my world had been characterized by a pervasive sense of dissatisfaction. Everything was a source of complaint. I was never genuinely happy. As my spiritual life deepened, I began to cultivate an awareness of the blessings in my life, no matter how small they seemed. It shifted my focus from seeing what was missing to seeing what was present.

I also found strength in connecting with others who shared similar spiritual paths. This interaction served as a constant reminder that I was a part of something larger than myself. My faith offered a narrative of hope, redemption, and inherent worth. Scriptures and preaching taught me that my struggles were not a reflection of my brokenness, but rather opportunities for growth and transformation.

This shift in attitude was a profound aspect of my spiritual awakening. The perils of the road while riding high will make one have a come-to-Jesus moment. I remember a time when I was driving in a storm, and a tornado was forming. I had to wait underneath a bridge for the tornado to pass over. I began talking to Jesus, and eventually, the storm ceased. Thank God, at that moment I was riding high His way and not with the monkey of addiction on my back. Another time, I was caught in a storm in the Arbuckle hills of Arkansas. The high winds were swinging my trailer from side to side. I immediately called on the name of Jesus, and suddenly the storm ceased. As an old spiritual says, "The winds and the waves shall obey His will. Peace, be still." In that very moment, I realized who was navigating on my behalf.

As I became more confident, I began to seek employment more aligned with my renewed sense of purpose. My spiritual awakening had awakened me to do remarkable things. This meant looking beyond simply securing a job and instead seeking out work that offered a sense of fulfillment. I found that in trucking! Finally, I was "riding high" in a positive light. After I searched and found my purpose in trucking, I went on to become a driving trainer instructor with the trucking company with which I was employed. I trained other drivers on how to drive for many years. I hold all endorsements. I am proficient in doubles and triples, hazmat, tankers, and oversized vehicles. With these endorsements, I became more valuable, which allowed me to be more selective when seeking advancement in the trucking industry.

My journey from addiction to recovery has been hard, but every hardship has made me stronger, wiser, and more compassionate. The scars remain, but they are now symbols of survival. Life after addiction is not perfect, but it is what it is, and it is mine. For anyone reading this, may my story encourage you to change. May you break free from addiction, embrace, and trust in your ability to overcome. In the depths of darkness, there is always a glimmer of light, and with courage, you can follow it to a new beginning. Always remember, God can take you from someplace to a no place, to a new place.

Personal Transformation

1. *In what ways have you experienced transformation after overcoming a major challenge or addiction?*

____

____

____

____

2. *How do you see yourself differently now compared to before your journey of overcoming began?*

____

____

____

____

Sources of Strength

1. *What spiritual practices, scriptures, or personal beliefs have given you strength during challenging times?*

____

____

____

____

2. *How have these sources helped you when you faced cravings, shame, or moments of weakness?*

____

____

____

____

Role of Community

1. *How has being part of a supportive community or faith group contributed to your recovery or personal growth?*

____

____

____

____

2. *Can you recall a time when someone in your community made a significant difference in your journey?*

____

____

____

____

Gratitude and Perspective

1. *How has practicing gratitude changed your outlook on life and recovery?*

____

____

____

____

2. *What are the small blessings or positive changes you have noticed since beginning your journey of overcoming?*

____

____

____

____

Purpose and Fulfillment

1. *Has your sense of purpose shifted because of overcoming adversity? If so, how?*

____

____

____

____

2. What new goals or dreams have emerged for you since your recovery began?

____

____

____

Helping Others

1. In what ways can you use your experiences to support or inspire others who are facing similar struggles?

____

____

____

____

2. What advice or encouragement would you offer to someone who is just starting their journey of overcoming?

____

____

____

____

Ongoing Challenges

1. What challenges do you still face, and how do you address them differently now?

____

____

____

____

2. How do you maintain hope and resilience when setbacks occur?

____

____

____

____

Faith and Identity

1. How has your relationship with God or your faith evolved through the process of overcoming?

____

____

____

____

2. *What scriptures or spiritual truths continue to anchor you as you move forward?*

____

____

____

____

Chapter 5:

The Spiritual Ascent

Let me tell you, rebuilding my life after addiction was not about getting a job; it was about finding a deeper connection, both with myself, God, and with the people around me.

As time went on, something shifted. Overcoming stopped feeling like a checklist and started to feel like a real relationship, with God, with my family, and with myself. It was not a dramatic moment, more like a slow sunrise. I would catch myself pausing during a busy day, just to breathe and feel that quiet presence, sometimes looking up at the sky. I started to sense that there was something bigger at work, something guiding me, even in the smallest moments.

My relationship with God changed, too. At first, I saw Him as a rescuer, someone who pulled me out of the pit. But as I grew, I realized He was more than that, He was a constant companion, always there, not just in crisis but in everyday life. It was like coming home to a truth I had always known but never really understood.

This new spiritual connection started to affect my relationships with others. I used to make decisions based on ego or the need for approval. Now, I found myself asking, "Does this feel right? Is this true to who I am becoming?" That shift made me more honest, more present, and more caring in my interactions.

The biggest change was in how I saw myself. For years, I was broken, unworthy of love. Addiction fed that lie. But discovering unconditional love, from God, from my wife, from my kids, helped me see myself differently. I started to forgive myself, not by ignoring my mistakes, but by accepting them as part of my journey. That self-forgiveness made it easier to forgive others, too.

Gratitude has become a daily practice. I would wake up and notice the little things: the hum of the fridge, the warmth of the sun, the taste of coffee. These small moments reminded me how far I had come. I would think about my family, my friends, and the support I received. Even the tough times became reminders of the grace that carried me through.

And let us talk about relationships. My connection with my wife deepened as I learned to be more open and vulnerable. We talked honestly about my struggles and dreams. With my kids, I tried to be present, to listen, and to show them that change is possible. I reached out to friends, old and new, sharing my story and listening to theirs. These relationships became my lifeline, reminding me that I was not alone.

At work, I started to see my job as more than just a paycheck. It was a chance to serve, to help others, and to live out my values. I became more dependable, more supportive, and more willing to lend a hand. The respect and trust I earned from colleagues felt like a real victory, proof that I was rebuilding not just my career, but my character.

I took a dedicated route from home every Sunday morning around 10:00 a.m. after praise and worship so that I could make it to my destination in Kansas City, Missouri, for my 6:00 a.m. delivery. The time spent worshiping before the trip really blessed me, and the travails of driving for extended periods of time.

I was also able to meet some great people while driving cross-country. I can remember times when I would be in Lufkin, Texas, and have an overnight stay. On my ten-hour break, there was a pastor and a deacon I met who would pick me up from the truck stop and bring me to Bible study, then return me to my truck. I have kept in touch with them over the years. These studies helped me stay grounded as an overcomer. I also found my spiritual ascent taking me to fellowship from time to time at Wednesday night Bible studies in different cities across the country.

Of course, there were challenges. Old habits did not disappear overnight. There were moments of doubt, times when I wanted to retreat. But I learned to return to that quiet place inside, to lean on my faith and my loved ones. Each time I did, I felt stronger, more centered.

The fruits of the Spirit, love, joy, peace, patience, kindness, goodness, faithfulness, gentleness, and self-control, started to show up in my life. I became more patient in disagreements and kinder to strangers. These were not just traits I tried to adopt; they grew naturally out of the peace I had found.

In the end, the quietude I discovered was not just the absence of chaos; it was a deep sense of belonging. I did not need external validation or the rush of a high to feel okay. I was finally at peace, anchored by faith, surrounded by love, and connected to the people who mattered most.

If you are reading this and wondering if real change is possible, I am here to tell you it is. Relationships, spiritual, family, friends, and even work, are the foundation. Lean into them. Be honest, be vulnerable, and let yourself be loved. That is where the real ascent begins.

REFLECTIONS

Spiritual Connection

1. *How has your relationship with God or your sense of spirituality changed during your journey of recovery?*

____

____

____

____

2. *Can you recall a moment when you felt a deeper connection or sense of guidance in your daily life? What was that experience like?*

____

____

____

____

Self-Forgiveness and Acceptance

1. *In what ways have you learned to forgive yourself for past mistakes? How has self-forgiveness impacted your healing?*

____

____

____

2. *What steps can you take to continue accepting yourself and your journey?*

____

____

____

Practicing Gratitude

1. *How has gratitude become a part of your daily routine? What small moments or blessings do you notice now that you may have overlooked before?*

____

____

____

____

2. *How does gratitude help you stay grounded and positive?*

____

____

____

Relationships and Community

1. *How have your relationships with family, friends, or colleagues changed as you have grown spiritually?*

____

____

____

____

2. *What role do honesty and vulnerability play in building stronger connections?*

____

____

____

____

Overcoming Challenges

1. *What challenges or old habits still arise for you? How do you use faith, community, or personal practices to overcome them?*

____

____

____

____

2. *What helps you return to a place of peace and strength when you feel doubt or temptation?*

Fruits of Spiritual Growth

1. *Which qualities (such as love, joy, peace, patience, kindness, goodness, faithfulness, gentleness, or self-control) have become more evident in your life?*

---

2. *How do these qualities influence your interactions with others?*

Finding Purpose and Belonging

1. *How has your sense of purpose evolved as you have rebuilt your life?*

____

____

____

____

2. *What does belonging mean to you now, and how do you nurture it in your life?*

____

____

____

____

Sharing Your Ascent

1. *In what ways can you share your story or support others who are seeking spiritual growth or recovery?*

____

____

____

____

2. *What message of hope or encouragement would you offer to someone beginning their own spiritual ascent?*

____

____

____

____

CHAPTER 6:

RIDING HIGH

At this point in my life, I am embracing success and navigating its challenges. Finally, I am riding high on life's true current. The phrase "riding high" evokes images of triumph, exhilaration, and a sense of being at the top of one's game. Whether in sports, personal achievements, or creative pursuits, reaching the pinnacle of success is a moment when all the hard work pays off and the rewards are tangible. But what does it truly mean to ride high, and what challenges and responsibilities come with this elevated position?

At its core, riding high is about experiencing a peak moment when confidence soars, obstacles seem surmountable, and goals appear within reach. For athletes, it might be the rush after scoring a winning goal; for entrepreneurs, it's closing a landmark deal; for artists, it's finally seeing their work recognized and appreciated; and for us truckers, it's the smile when the recipient receives the delivery they have so anxiously awaited. This surge of positivity fuels further motivation, inspiring individuals to push boundaries and set even higher ambitions. For me, it is doing what I do best: driving!

The road to success did not come easy. Before a person can ride high, there are often months or years of dedication, sacrifice, and resilience. The journey is rarely smooth. Setbacks, failures, and moments of doubt are integral parts of the process. Those who finally reach a high point have not only honed their skills but also cultivated a mindset capable of enduring the lows. Thus, riding high is not just about the destination; it reflects the journey and the personal growth achieved along the way. Going from someplace to a no place to a new place is an exhilarating feeling. I had to let go of the stinking thinking for it to work.

I have learned to maintain perspective while riding high. Grounding oneself through gratitude, humility, and self-awareness helps ensure that riding high does not become overwhelming or isolating. The true strength of riding high lies not just in how one manages success, but in how one faces adversity when it inevitably comes. The "high" I experience now is not fleeting but a deep, abiding sense of contentment and gratitude that saturates my entire being. It is a quiet joy that arises from the simple act of being present, from appreciating the beauty of the mundane, and from knowing that I am living a life that is authentic to myself. This abiding peace is the ultimate high state of being that transcends all external circumstances and offers a profound, unshakable joy.

Many of us, knowingly or not, swim upstream. We resist change, cling to comfort zones, or try to control outcomes. This resistance can lead to frustration, exhaustion, and a sense of being stuck. To ride high on life's current is to release that resistance, to trust the process, to accept uncertainty, and to allow ourselves to be carried by the flow. This does not mean being passive but rather being engaged with life that is rooted in openness and resilience.

Being present is essential to feeling the current. When we are attentive to the present moment, we are more attuned to the subtle shifts in our mood, environment, and relationships. Spending time with my children, grandchildren, and great-grandchildren now affords me this opportunity.

I have truly learned to live in the moment and am enjoying every minute. Living in the moment brings peace, grounding us in the now rather than pulling us into the past or propelling us into the future.

Purpose drives us towards our destiny. When our goals and actions reflect our values, life feels meaningful and satisfying. Take time to reflect: What brings you joy? What issues ignite your passion? Who do you hope to be, not just in the eyes of others but to yourself? When you clarify your "why," it will carry you towards your highest potential.

Even when following the current, life brings both peaceful stretches and some storms. The key is to embrace both. In times of calm, save it for serenity and use it to recharge. In moments of chaos, remember that turbulence is temporary. The current, steadfast and true, continues beneath the surface. Trust that these challenges are part of the journey, often leading to growth, insight, and unexpected opportunities.

Riding high means not only moving forward but also celebrating the ride. Seek out experiences that delight you, cultivate relationships that nourish your soul, and make time for play, laughter, and rest. Authentic joy is found in the moments we let ourselves be fully alive, unburdened by the pretense of fear. It is the laughter with friends, the satisfaction of a hard day's work, and the peace of a sunset at day's end.

To ride high on life's true current is to live courageously, authentically, and with gratitude. It is the trust and the wisdom of your inner self to accept the journey as it unfolds, and to savor both the adventure and the quiet. By honoring your true current, you move beyond mere existence; you thrive, inspired and awake, riding each wave with purpose and joy.

Riding high is an exhilarating experience, full of energy and promise. But it is also a time of introspection, responsibility, and preparation for the future. By embracing the joys and confronting the challenges of riding high, you can make the most of your peak moments, using them as opportunities for growth, inspiration, and lasting impact.

My renewed relationship with God drives my commitment to living a life of purpose. It is about more than just abstaining from destructive behaviors; it is about actively constructing a life filled with meaning and contribution. This involves identifying what truly ignites my spirit, what passions I can pursue, and how I can serve others in ways that align with my gifts and my experiences. Whether it is through sharing my story, mentoring others on their overcoming journey, or simply engaging in acts of kindness in my daily life, each purposeful action reinforces the sense of fulfillment and gratitude that permeates my existence.

After all the years of adventures driving cross-country, my wife and I came to an agreement that it was time for me to be off the road. We prayed for God to open a door where I could drive locally and be home every day. What is great about God is that He can open any door, at any time, and He did just that! I am enjoying my best life, riding high on life's true current.

Experiencing Success

1. *What does "riding high" mean to you personally? Can you recall a moment when you felt enormously successful or at the peak of your abilities?*

____

____

____

____

2. *How did you reach that point, and what challenges did you overcome along the way?*

____

____

____

____

Maintaining Perspective

1. *How do you stay grounded when experiencing success or positive momentum in life?*

____

____

____

2. *What practices or attitudes help you maintain humility and gratitude during high points?*

____

____

____

Authentic Joy vs. Fleeting Highs

1. *How does the "high" you experience now differ from past moments of artificial or fleeting happiness?*

____

____

____

2. *What brings you deep, lasting contentment today?*

____

____

____

Navigating Life's Current

1.   In what ways do you resist or go with the flow of life's changes?

____

____

____

____

2.   How do you practice trust and openness when facing uncertainty or turbulence?

____

____

____

____

Being Present

1.   What helps you stay mindful and attentive to the present moment?

____

____

____

____

2. How does practicing presence affect your mood, relationships, and sense of peace?

____

____

____

Purpose and Direction

1. What is your "why," the purpose or passion that guides your actions?

____

____

____

2. How do you clarify and pursue your goals so they align with your values?

____

____

____

Embracing Both Calm and Chaos

1. How do you handle both tranquil and turbulent times in your life?

____

____

____

____

2. What strategies help you recharge during calm periods and persevere through chaos?

____

____

____

____

Celebrating the Ride

1. What experiences, relationships, or activities bring you authentic joy?

____

____

____

____

2. How do you make time to celebrate your progress and savor the present?

____

____

____

Living with Intention

1. How do you actively construct a life filled with meaning and contribution?

____

____

____

2. What passions or gifts can you pursue to serve others and reinforce your sense of fulfillment?

____

____

____

Preparing for the Future

1. *What responsibilities or preparations come with success?*

____

____

____

____

2. *How do you use your peak moments as platforms for growth, inspiration, and lasting impact?*

____

____

____

____

About the Author

Bruce C. Rucker, Sr., is a veteran trucking specialist. His call was initially to drive trucks. Trucking is in his blood. Bruce always desired freedom and adventure. He began his career as a long-haul driver. Bruce has been a professional driver for over 29 years. His experience includes over-the-road, regional, dedicated, and local driving. In addition, he has experience with heavy equipment, oversized permit loads, dry vans, refrigerated vans, and flatbed trucks.

Bruce is also proficient in hazmat, doubles, and triple tankers. He holds all endorsements in the trucking industry. Additionally, he has achieved the three-million-mile safe driving award. Bruce has driven in 48 states in the United States and has also driven in Canada. Bruce has also been a driving instructor/trainer in the industry. Bruce believes, "Your gift makes room for you." He is happily married to his wife of 28 years, has four children, and is a proud grandfather and great-grandfather.

9 781970 816105